Comedians' Quote Book

Comedians' Quote Book

Quick Takes from the Great Comics

**MERRIT MALLOY &
MARSHA ROSE**

 Sterling Publishing Co., Inc. New York

Library of Congress Cataloging-in-Publication Data

Comedians' quote book : quick takes from the great
  comics / [compiled] by Merrit Malloy and Marsha Rose.
      p.   cm.
  Includes index.
  ISBN 0-8069-0324-4
    1. Quotations, English.   2. American wit and humor.
I. Malloy, Merrit.   II. Rose, Marsha.
  PN6081.C85   1993
  081—dc20   92-41346
                                                   CIP

10   9   8   7   6   5   4   3   2   1

Published in 1993 by Sterling Publishing Company, Inc.
387 Park Avenue South, New York, N.Y. 10016
© 1993 by Porosan Group
Distributed in Canada by Sterling Publishing
% Canadian Manda Group, P.O. Box 920, Station U
Toronto, Ontario, Canada M8Z 5P9
Distributed in Great Britain and Europe by Cassell PLC
Villiers House, 41/47 Strand, London WC2N 5JE, England
Distributed in Australia by Capricorn Link Ltd.
P.O. Box 665, Lane Cove, NSW 2066
Manufactured in the United States of America
All rights reserved

Sterling ISBN 0-8069-0324-4

The compilers would like to thank our staff and researchers for their invaluable assistance. In particular, we'd like to thank Ron Ellis, who did much of the comedy-quote research and provided editorial assistance throughout; Molly Malloy Wiest, who spent her whole summer vacation at our computer, adding these comedy quotes to our database; Rick Rose, who set up our database system and kept it up and running, despite our ongoing growth and increasing demands; WordPerfect wizard Randy Reynaldo, who rescued us from an editorial logjam; Bob Westal, who typed and edited the final draft; Nancy Lindsey, our reliable, good-natured friend, who often stepped in as a pinch hitter; and Rosie Chavez, of our permanent staff, who maintained our offices and lifted our spirits.

And finally, as always, we're grateful to THE FUR PEOPLE for their subtle indifference towards our work, which provides us with the needed daily reminder not to take ourselves too seriously.

Contents

Introduction

Current quotes and quips from the funniest people alive! The best and the brightest stand-up comics are included here: Bob Rickman, Cassandra Davis, Pauly Shore of MTV, and Rick Reynolds, as well as our most gifted reliables— Bill Cosby, Richard Pryor, Flip Wilson, Carol Burnett, Steve Martin, Rodney Dangerfield, Roseanne Barr-Arnold, Jerry Seinfeld, Garry Shandling, Joan Rivers, Larry Miller, Jackie Mason, and Phyllis Diller. Literary humorists are included, from Art Buchwald, Erma Bombeck, and Andy Rooney to A. Whitney Brown (formerly of "Saturday Nite Live"), Fran Lebowitz and Carrie Snow (two of the best in quick wit and current cynicism), and Garrison Keillor (well known for his easy hometown humor). Cartoonists are here, from the legendary Charles Schulz and Jules Feiffer to Garry Trudeau, Cathy Guisewite, Gary Larson, and others. Here are our most prolific "comedy giants," beginning with veterans like Bob Hope, Milton Berle, George Burns, and Johnny Carson, to biting up-to-the-minute comedians like Jay Leno, David Letterman, Pat Sajak and Dennis Miller, and provocative geniuses like Lily Tomlin, Robin Williams, and Steven Wright. Our most gifted current playwrights are included—Neil Simon, Larry Gelbart, Wendy Wasserman and Jane Wagner. Political commentators with searing wit, like Mort Sahl, P.J. O'Rourke, Calvin Trillin, and Dave Barry are all here. Outrageously funny screen and television writers, including Woody

Allen, Mel Brooks, Nora Ephron, Billy Wilder, Carl Reiner, Diane English, Linda Bloodworth-Thomason, Gary David Goldberg, Susan Harris, and Pat McCormick also appear. And, finally, from the archives, some of the real treasures of comedy are here—Jack Benny, Gracie Allen, Red Skelton, Ernie Kovacs, Fred Allen, W.C. Fields, Mae West, Victor Borge, Sam Levenson, the inimitable Bishop Fulton J. Sheen, and (of course) Lucy and Groucho.

We may not live in a funny world, but we do live in a world of funny people—funny and often deeply wise. Because of them, whatever happens, we learn not to take it all too seriously, because, as Jane Wagner puts it, ". . . no matter how cynical you become, it's never enough to keep up."

Advice

Never trust a naked bus driver.

—Jack Douglas

Never lend your car to anyone to whom you have given birth.

—Erma Bombeck

Never get into fights with ugly people, because they have nothing to lose.

—Unknown

Never thank anybody for anything, except for a drink of water in the desert—and then make it brief.

—Gene Fowler

Never wear polyester underwear if you're going to be hit by lightning.

—Roz, "Cheers"

Radar, don't pick at your food; it won't heal.

—Hawkeye Pierce "M*A*S*H"

Never floss a stranger.

—Joan Rivers

Try everything in life except incest and square dancing.

—George S. Kaufman

Never go to bed mad. Stay up and fight.

—**Phyllis Diller**

Never moon a werewolf!

—**Mike Binder**

If you use a waffle iron for a pillow, be sure it's unplugged.

—**Gary Owens**

Buy thermometers in the wintertime. They're much lower then.

—**Soupy Sales**

Never eat more than you can lift.

—**Miss Piggy**

Honey, get off the cross. Somebody else needs the wood.

—**Dolly Parton in** *Straight Talk*

Aging

If I'd known I was going to live this long, I'd have taken better care of myself.

—**Jimmy Durante**

Retirement must be wonderful. I mean, you can suck in your stomach for only so long.

—**Burt Reynolds**

There's one advantage to being one hundred and two. There's no peer pressure.

—**Dennis Wolfberg**

Crossing the street in New York keeps old people going—if they make it.

—**Andy Rooney**

The best way to be young is to hang out with old people.

—**Nipsey Russell**

You're only young once—and if you work it right—once is enough!

—**Joe E. Lewis**

I recently turned fifty, which is young for a tree, mid-life for an elephant, and ancient for a quarter-miler whose son now says, "Dad, I just can't run with you anymore unless I bring something to read."

—**Bill Cosby**

I have reached an age when I look as good standing on my head as I do right side up.

—**Frank Sullivan**

Just remember, once you're over the hill, you begin to pick up speed.

—**Charles Schulz**

Don't worry about avoiding temptation. As you grow older, it will avoid you.

—Joey Adams

My mother always used to say: "The older you get, the better you get—unless you're a banana."

—Rose Nylund, "The Golden Girls"

Women, don't get a tattoo. That butterfly looks great on your breast when you're twenty or thirty, but when you get to be seventy, it stretches into a condor."

—Billy Elmer

I'm thirty-six—three years older than Jesus was—so I've gotta watch my step now.

—Kathy Ladman

You know you're getting old when you don't care where your wife goes, just so you don't have to go along.

—Jacob Braude

"Don't worry about senility," my grandfather used to say. "When it hits you, you won't know it."

—Bill Cosby

It's a sobering thought that when Mozart was my age, he had been dead for two years."

—Tom Lehrer

The only real way to look younger is not to be born so soon.

—Charles Schulz

America

We're America's worst nightmare. White trash with money!

—Tom Arnold, husband of Roseanne Barr

Soon after I came to America, I went to Tennessee. They are always checking your hearing there. They keep saying, "Now, you come back. You hear?"

—Yakov Smirnoff

I am from Osaka, Japan. I came to America because I'm lazy.

—Teliho Hasuki

Celebrity in America is extraordinary. It's like being in the Royal Family. It amazes me. They think you can cure cancer.

—Tracey Ullman

[America] is the only country in the world where failing to promote yourself is regarded as being arrogant.

—Garry Trudeau

America is the only country where it takes more brains to make out the income-tax return than it does to make the income.

—Jacob Braude

There's three moments in a man's life: when he buys a house, a car, and a new color TV. That's what America is all about.

—Archie Bunker, "All in the Family"

Land of my dreams—home of the Whopper.

—Balki Bartokomous, "Perfect Strangers"

If you speak three languages, you are trilingual. If you speak two languages, you are bilingual. If you speak one language, you're American.

—Sonny Spoon

Americans are a broad-minded people. They'll accept the fact that a person can be an alcoholic, a dope fiend, a wife beater, and even a newspaperman, but if a man doesn't drive, there's something wrong with him.

—Art Buchwald

["The Simpsons"] represent the American family in all its horror.

—Matt Groening, creator of "The Simpsons"

This country is so urbanized we think low-fat milk comes from cows on aerobic-exercise programs.

—P. J. O'Rourke

Animals

All creatures must learn to coexist. That's why the brown bear and the field mouse can share their lives and live in harmony. Of course, they can't mate or the mice would explode.

—Rose Nylund, "The Golden Girls"

16

Have you ever noticed that mice don't have shoulders?

—**George Carlin**

Curiosity killed the cat, but for a while I was a suspect.

—**Steven Wright**

Cats are intended to teach us that not everything in nature has a purpose.

—**Garrison Keillor**

The problem with cats is that they get the exact same look for a moth or an ax murderer.

—**Paula Poundstone**

[To Dreyfus, the dog] You're glad to see me every minute of my life. I come home, you jump around and wag your tail. I go in the closet, I come out, you jump around and wag your tail. I turn my face away, I turn it back, you wag your tail. Either you love me very much or your short-term memory is shot.

—**Dr. Harry Weston, "Empty Nest"**

Sending a bill to a duck is even more redundant than dying in Philadelphia.

—**Sister Mary Tricky**

Outside of a dog, a book is man's best friend. Inside of a dog, it's too dark to read.

—**Groucho Marx**

Did you ever see a homeless person with a dog? The dog's probably thinking, "Hey, I don't need this guy, I can do this by myself."

—**Norm McDonald**

They say the dog is man's best friend. I don't believe that. How many of your friends have you neutered?

—**Larry Reeb**

If cats could talk, they would lie to you.

—**Rob Kopack**

You can lead a horse to water—but before you push him in, just stop and think how a wet horse smells.

—**George Gobel**

I heard about an educated chimp at the zoo who read Darwin's *On the Origin of Species* and said, "Good gracious, am I my keeper's brother?"

—**Larry Wilde**

It's great to have a dog in the city. When you go out for a walk, he protects you from muggers you would never get to see if you didn't have to take this dog for a walk!

—**Unknown**

Did you ever notice that when you blow into a dog's face he gets mad, but when you take him in a car he sticks his head out the window?

—**Steve Bluestein**

I just bought a Chihuahua. It's the dog for lazy people. You don't have to walk it. Just hold it out the window and squeeze.

—**Anthony Clark**

Due to the shape of the North American elk's esophagus, even if it could speak, it could not pronounce the word "lasagna."

—**Cliff Clavin, "Cheers"**

Pets are nature's way of reminding us that, in the incredibly complex ecological chain of life, there is no room for furniture.

—Dave Barry

Beauty

Just be considerate, accept each other for what you are, and don't point out the fact that the hair he's losing on his head is now growing out of his nose—and his ears.

—Peg Bundy, "Married with Children"

Beauty is only skin deep, but ugly goes clear to the bone.

—Unknown

The most common error made in matters of appearance is the belief that one should disdain the superficial and let the true beauty of one's soul shine through. If there are places on your body where this is a possibility, you are not attractive—you are leaking.

—Fran Lebowitz

Remember always that the least-plain sister is the family beauty.

—George Bernard Shaw

Did you ever have one of those nights when you didn't want to go out, but your hair looked too good to stay home?

—**Jack Simmons**

You'd be surprised how much it costs to look this cheap.

—**Dolly Parton**

Never purchase beauty products in hardware stores.

—**Miss Piggy**

A thing of beauty is a job forever.

—**Milton Berle**

Yogi Berra

Baseball is ninety-percent mental, and the other half is physical.

—**Yogi Berra**

Déjà vu all over again.

—**Yogi Berra**

It gets late early out there.

—**Yogi Berra**

(When asked what time it was) You mean right now?

—**Yogi Berra**

Nobody goes to that restaurant anymore. It's too crowded.

—**Yogi Berra**

A baseball official's wife met Yogi Berra and said that he looked like a pretty "cool" fellow. And Yogi replied, "You don't look so hot yourself!"

—**Richard Nixon**

Always go to other people's funerals, otherwise they won't come to yours.

—**Yogi Berra**

That's his style of hittin'. If you can't imitate him, don't copy him.

—**Yogi Berra**

If the people don't want to come out to the park, nobody's gonna stop them.

—**Yogi Berra**

It ain't over till it's over.

—**Yogi Berra**

Birth

Somewhere on this globe every ten seconds, there is a woman giving birth to a child. She must be found and stopped.

—**Sam Levenson**

I had a Jewish delivery. They knock you out at the first pain and wake you up when the hairdresser shows.

—**Joan Rivers**

My mother's version of natural childbirth was . . . she took off her makeup.

—**Rita Rudner**

My wife—God bless her—was in labor for thirty-two hours, and I was faithful to her the entire time.

—**Jonathan Katz**

I've laid several eggs, but only two have been fertilized.

—**Ernestyne White**

Having a baby is like taking your lower lip and forcing it over your head.

—**Carol Burnett**

Birth Control

That's why I still take the Pill. I don't want any more grandchildren.

—**Phyllis Diller**

A vasectomy is never having to say you're sorry.

—**Rubin Carson**

I was involved in an extremely good example of oral contraception two weeks ago. I asked a girl to go to bed with me and she said no.

—**Woody Allen**

The best contraceptive for old people is nudity.

—**Phyllis Diller**

Bodies

God did not create this package to work.

—**Kelly Bundy, "Married with Children"**

I knew I got a bargain for this dress when I heard a lady tell someone that I had gotten it for a ridiculous figure.

—**Minnie Pearl**

The reason I don't sign the organ-donor part of my driver's license is that I can imagine an accident where I'm badly injured and a very large cop is standing over me whose uncle needs a kidney.

—**Lou Schneider**

When I die, I'm going to leave my body to science fiction.

—**Steven Wright**

I'm getting very comfortable with my body. I love sleeping on a full-length mirror.

—**Sandra Bernhard**

I went to the beach today, and I could feel the women dressing me with their eyes.

—**Bob Nickman**

Bumper Stickers

Congressional corruption: a renewable resource

Men are animals, but they make great pets.

Adam was a rough draft.

Get even. Live long enough to be a problem to your kids.

Don't tell me what kind of day to have.

God loves you and I'm trying.

If you don't like the way I drive, get off the sidewalk.

If you love someone, set them free. If they don't come back, hunt them down and kill them.

Engineers know all the angles.

I feel like such a failure. I've been shopping for over twenty years, and I still have nothing to wear.

Of all the things I miss, the thing I miss the most is my mind.

A woman's place is in the mall.

It's been lovely, but I have to scream now.

I brake for insights.

—**Lotus Weinstock**

George Burns

Sex can be fun after eighty, after ninety, and after lunch!

—**George Burns**

Don't stay in bed . . . unless you make money in bed.

—**George Burns**

Happiness is having a large, loving, caring close-knit family in another city.

—**George Burns**

I made the seeds too big.

—George Burns (As God, regarding avocados)

In show business the key word is honesty. Once you've learned to fake that, the rest is easy.

—George Burns

At my age, I don't even buy green bananas.

—George Burns

People keep asking me how it feels to be ninety-five, and I tell them I feel just as good as I did when I was ninety-four.

—George Burns

Tonight we honor a man old enough to be his own father . . . a man who embarrassed everyone at the Last Supper by asking for seconds.

—Red Buttons

I was always taught to respect my elders, and I've now reached the age when I don't have anybody to respect.

—George Burns

I can't die now—I'm booked.

—George Burns

Business

We make money the old-fashioned way—we borrow it.

—Stockbroker, "Barney Miller"

Progress might have been all right once, but it's gone on too long.

—Ogden Nash

Did you ever hear of a kid playing accountant—even if he wanted to be one?

—Jackie Mason

I sold my house this week. I got a pretty good price for it, but it made my landlord mad as hell.

—Garry Shandling

There are two times in a man's life when he shouldn't speculate: when he can't afford it and when he can.

—Mark Twain

If there was any justice in this world, oil-company executive bathrooms would smell like the ones in their gas stations.

—Johnny Carson

We don't care. We don't have to. We're the phone company.

—Ernestine the operator, "Laugh-In"

All those who enjoy making pirate sounds, say, "Aye!"
All those who enjoy making horse sounds, say, "Nay!"

—Cartoonist Callahan

Bankruptcy is a proceeding in which you put your money in your pants pocket and give your coat to your creditors.

—Joey Adams

In Japan we know how to save face and always look smart. If someone rips you off in America, you say, "He's a jerk." In Japan, we say, "Oh, he's a business genius. He should be working for our company!"

—Tamayo Otsuki

The President asked the Japanese, "Why don't you buy more American cars?" The Japanese answered, "Why don't *you* buy more American cars?"

—Bill Maher

California

I love California. I grew up in Phoenix.

—Dan Quayle

I mean, who would want to live in a place where the only cultural advantage is that you can turn right on a red light?

—Woody Allen

There are two million interesting people in New York and only seventy-eight in Los Angeles.

—Neil Simon

In California everyone goes to a therapist, is a therapist, or is a therapist going to a therapist.

—Truman Capote

Los Angeles is the only place where people list CAT scans as film credits on their résumé.

—Dennis Miller

San Francisco is a wild place. A sort of human game preserve.

—Robin Williams

Los Angeles is a great place. Where else can you smell the air and see it coming at you at the same time!

—Jackie Gayle

Californians are health-conscious. They think it's bad luck to spill salt substitute.

—Johnny Carson

The more someone dislikes California, the more likely he or she is from an eastern state. The more extreme the dislike, the more likely he or she is from Ohio.

—E. Garrison

A California company has invented a new revolutionary light bulb that will last up to 20,000 hours. That's kind of depressing, isn't it, to know a California light bulb lasts longer than a California marriage? You could be on your third marriage and still be on your first light bulb.

—Jay Leno

Fall is my favorite season in Los Angeles, watching the birds change colors and fall from the trees.

—**David Letterman**

Perhaps there's no life after death . . . there's just Los Angeles.

—**Rick Anderson**

Children

"I figure if the kids are alive at the end of the day, I've done my job."

—**Roseanne Barr-Arnold**

Little stupid people who don't pay rent.

—**Rick Reynolds**

The first thing a child learns when he gets a drum is that he is never going to get another one.

—**Ann Landers**

You can usually count on kids to quote you correctly, especially if it's something you wish you hadn't said.

—**Jesse Andrews**

Having a baby is like living with a vampire. They sleep by day and suck the life out of you at night.

—**Bobby Slayton**

By all means, tell your child about sex—but be honest— use books, diagrams, and a laugh track.

—**Sheldon Keller**

Adults are always asking little kids what they want to be when they grow up—'cause they're looking for ideas.

—**Paula Poundstone**

I always wondered why babies spend so much time sucking their thumbs. Then I tasted that baby food!

—**Robert Orben**

You know your children are growing up when they stop asking you where they came from and refuse to tell you where they're going.

—**P. O'Brien**

When I was a kid, my parents moved a lot—but I always found them.

—**Rodney Dangerfield**

Frank Zappa named his daughter Moon Unit. And everybody knows that's a boy's name.

—**John Hinton, KLOS "5 O'Clock Funnies"**

Parents were invented to make children happy by giving them something to ignore.

—**Ogden Nash**

Kids—they're not easy, but there has to be some penalty for sex!

—**Bill Maher**

They're all mine. . . . Of course, I'd trade any one of them for a dishwasher.

—**Roseanne Barr-Arnold**

When you're in fifth grade and faced with having to choose between eternal life and recess, eternal life doesn't stand a chance.

—**Tony Vanaria**

Communication

I wish people who have trouble communicating would just shut up.

—**Tom Lehrer**

It's a rare person who wants to hear what he doesn't want to hear.

—**Dick Cavett**

Many are called, but few are called back.

—**Sister Mary Tricky**

Courage

I was right where the bullets were thickest—underneath the ammunition truck.

—**Lou Costello**

Kamikaze pilots had to do all of their bragging ahead of time.

—**Tommy Sledge**

A coward dies a hundred deaths, a brave man only once. . . . But then, once is enough, isn't it?

—**Judge Harry Stone, "Night Court"**

I'd feel a lot braver if I wasn't so scared.

—**Hawkeye Pierce, "M*A*S*H"**

If God wanted us to be brave, why did He give us legs?

—**Marvin Kitman**

Screw up your courage. You screwed up everything else.

—**Donald Smith**

Crime

It's a proven fact that capital punishment is a known de-tergent for crime.

—**Archie Bunker, "All in the Family"**

A kleptomaniac is a person who helps himself because he can't help himself.

—**Henry Morgan**

I think my mistake was yelling, "Hi!" to the witnesses as they filed into court.

—**Phil Interlandi**

I'm getting a little worried about our neighborhood-watch program. Some guy called and woke me at 3 A.M. to let me know that there was a little piece of saliva running down the side of my mouth.

—**Harland Williams**

Cynicism

I worry that no matter how cynical you become, it's never enough to keep up.

—**Jane Wagner**

Never accept an invitation from a stranger unless he offers you candy.

—**Linda Festa**

The trouble with being in the rat race is that even if you win, you're still a rat.

—**Lily Tomlin**

When something good happens, it's a miracle, and you should wonder what God is saving up for you later.

—**Marshall Brickman**

The only reason some people get lost in thought is because it's unfamiliar territory.

—**Paul Fix**

The cost of livin's going up, and the chance of livin's going down.

—**Flip Wilson**

A good deed never goes unpunished.

—**Gore Vidal**

Moonlight is romantic, but it's hell to read by.

—**Remington Steele, "Remington Steele"**

The world gets better every day, then worse again in the evening.

—**Kin Hubbard**

The power of accurate observation is commonly called cynicism by those who have not got it.

—**George Bernard Shaw**

There's nothing like a hardship song to set my toes a-tapping.

—Roseanne Barr-Arnold

Dating

I know I'm not Mr. Right, but . . . would you settle for Mr. Right Now?

—From the cartoon "Quigmans"

Dating is an ancient ritual where, over a long series of consecutive, romantic dinners, you work very hard to be fascinating, witty, and charming so that you eventually get married and never speak to each other over dinner again!

—Marsha Doble

I'm kind of lazy. I'm dating a pregnant woman.

—Ron Richards

A date is a job interview that lasts all night. The only difference between a date and a job interview is that there are not many job interviews where there's a chance you'll end up naked at the end of it.

—Jerry Seinfeld

I took up a collection for a man in our office. But I didn't get enough money to buy one.

—**Ruth Buzzi**

It's still fun to be single. You just have to be more careful. Your date comes to the door, you say, "I'm sewing this button on my jacket—oops, pricked your finger—I'll get a slide."

—**Elayne Boosler**

I went on a date. I said, "I like you, but can we just boil ourselves before we get into bed?"

—**Richard Lewis**

On a date, when I'm driving her home . . . this is when I wonder if there is going to be any sex—and if I'm going to be involved.

—**Garry Shandling**

I met this guy who said he loved children. Then I found out he was on parole for it.

—**Monica Piper**

Whenever I want a really nice meal, I start dating again.

—**Susan Healey**

I was dating this girl for two years, and right away the nagging starts: "I wanna know your name!"

—**Mike Binder**

I'm dating a homeless woman. It was easier to talk her into staying over.

—**Garry Shandling**

I don't mind men who kiss and tell. I need all the publicity I can get!

—**Ruth Buzzi**

I went out with Siamese twins, and my friend asked me if I had a good time. I said, "Yes and no!"

—**Dick Havilland**

I went to a computer dating service—and they gave me the number of Dial-a-Prayer.

—**Joey Bishop**

Death

You begin to grow up the moment you die.

—**Graffito**

Death is like sleep without the long-term commitment.

—**Lea Krinsky**

If there's a bullet out there with my name on it, that's okay—it's my time. It's the ones that say "To whom it may concern" that worry me.

—**Rob Fields**

I don't mind death. I just don't want to be there when it happens.

—**Woody Allen**

In the Jewish religion, we bury our dead before the next sunset. Which is civilized. They ain't going to get no better.

—**Alan King**

Everyone is afraid of dying alone. I don't understand. Who wants to die and have to be polite at the same time?

—**Quentin Crisp**

I believe in reincarnation, so in my will I'm leaving everything to myself.

—**Unknown**

For three days after death, hair and fingernails continue to grow but phone calls taper off.

—**Johnny Carson**

The great thing about suicide is that it's not one of those things you have to do now or you'll lose your chance. I mean, you can always do it later.

—**Harvey Fierstein**

My uncle's funeral cost $5,000—so far. We buried him in a rented tuxedo.

—**Dave Madden**

People always say "He died penniless," as if it's a terrible thing. Sounds like good timing to me.

—**Al Cleathen**

Either this man is dead or my watch has stopped.

—Groucho Marx

Definitions

I used to think I was poor. They told me it was self-defeating to think of myself as "needy." I was "deprived." Then they told me "underprivileged" was overused. I was "disadvantaged." I still don't have a dime, but now I have a great vocabulary.

—Jules Feiffer

A friend is a person who has the same enemies you have.

—Stephen Leacock

In English, my name means "very skinny black man." In African, it means "lion appetizer."

—Lahia Fahnbullen

Realtors are people who did not make it as used-car salesmen.

—Bob Newhart

Sex drive is a physical craving that begins in adolescence and ends at marriage.

—Robert Byrne

Wives are people who feel they don't dance enough.

—**Groucho Marx**

A bachelor is a man who never makes the same mistake once.

—**Ed Wynn**

My Uncle Murray said, "You're a man if you can make love as long as it takes to cook a chicken."

—**David Steinberg**

After all, what is reality anyway? Nothin' but a collective hunch.

—**Jane Wagner**

. . . a schizophrenic with low self-esteem . . . he thinks he's one person.

—**"Phoebe's Place" cartoon, by Bill Schorr**

A eunuch is a man who has had his works cut out for him.

—**Robert Byrne**

Life is what happens to you when you are making other plans.

—**John Lennon**

A narcissist is someone better looking than you are.

—**Gore Vidal**

A vegetarian is a person who won't eat anything that can have children.

—**David Brenner**

I think onstage nudity is disgusting, shameful, and damaging to all things American. But if I were twenty-two with a great body, it would be artistic, tasteful, patriotic, and a progressive religious experience.

—**Shelley Winters**

Bookie: A pickpocket who lets you use your own hands.

—**Henry Morgan**

Horse sense is the thing a horse has that keeps him from betting on people.

—**Herbert Swope**

Destiny is what you are supposed to do in life. Fate is what kicks you in the ass to do it.

—**Henry Miller**

Gossip is when you hear something you like about someone you don't!

—**Earl Wilson**

An intellectual is someone who can listen to the *William Tell* Overture and not think of the Lone Ranger.

—**Unknown**

Rich people are just poor people with money.

—**Sister Mary Tricky**

Stress—that confusion created when the mind must override the body's basic desire to choke the living • • • out of some idiot who desperately needs it.

—**Sign in an office**

Lawyer: Individual whose principal role is to protect his clients from other members of his profession.

—Bumper sticker

Infinity. It could be time on an ego trip, for all I know.

—Jane Wagner

Diet

I've been dieting for a week, and all I've lost is seven days.

—Pat Partridge

I went to a conference for bulimics and anorexics. It was a nightmare. The bulimics ate the anorexics.

—Monica Piper

I hate skinny women, especially when they say things like, "Sometimes I forget to eat." Now . . . I've forgotten my mother's maiden name . . . I've forgotten my car keys . . . but you've got to be a special kind of stupid to forget to eat.

—Marsha Warfield

I knew it was time to lose weight when my bathtub started getting stretch marks!

—Rodney Dangerfield

The best way to lose weight is to get the flu and take a trip to Egypt.

—**Roz Lawrence**

I never worry about diets. The only carrots that interest me are the number you get in a diamond.

—**Mae West**

It's not nice to make fun of fat people—but, what the hell, they can't catch you.

—**Marsha Warfield**

I'm so neurotic that I worry I'll lose weight when I'm on a diet.

—**Grace Hodgson**

The two biggest sellers in any bookstore are the cookbooks and the diet books. The cookbooks tell you how to prepare the food, and the diet books tell you how not to eat any of it.

—**Andy Rooney**

Divorce

For a while, we pondered whether to take a vacation or get a divorce. We decided that a trip to Bermuda is over in two weeks, but a divorce is something you always have.

—**Woody Allen**

Alimony is like putting gas into another guy's car.

—Milton Berle

The difference between divorce and legal separation is that a legal separation gives a husband time to hide his money.

—Johnny Carson

It equals out. I pay alimony to Laurie and Denise. And I get alimony from Brenda and Suzanne.

—From a cartoon by Sharris

My husband's going through his mid-life crisis. He left me for an *older* woman! What does she have that I don't, except osteoporosis and orthopedic shoes? If he would've waited ten years, I could have given him those.

—Eileen Finney

Couple stays together nine years after divorce—because they couldn't tell the DOGS! (Headline)

—Dean Farrell

Divorce is painful. There's an easy way to save yourself a lot of trouble. Just find a woman you hate and buy her a house!

—Pat Paulsen

Did you ever stop to think that paying alimony is like keeping up the payments on a car with four flats?

—Dan Rowan

God made men. God made women. And when God found that men could not get along with women, God invented Mexico.

—Larry Storch

45

Divorce can be painful, especially dividing things up: "You take the dog's hind legs and I'll take the front; you take the kid from the kidneys up and I'll take the rest."

—**Robert Klein**

Ed McMahon just received a letter from his ex-wife that said, "You may have already *lost* ten million dollars!"

—**Lahia Fahnbullen**

My parents are getting divorced, and my girlfriend and I don't know who to live with. My mom wants us to live with her, but my dad wants just my girlfriend to live with him.

—**Kirk Nolan**

Doctors

A male gynecologist is like an auto mechanic who never owned a car.

—**Carrie Snow**

If penicillin is such a wonder drug, then how come it can't cure bread mold?

—**Ron Smith**

There's nothing wrong with you that an expensive operation can't prolong.

—Graham Chapman

Some tortures are physical and some are mental, but the one that is both is dental.

—Ogden Nash

I don't like going to the dentist. I don't like having any part of a man in my mouth for that long.

—Martin Mull

My first psychiatrist said I was paranoid, but I wanted a second opinion because I think he was out to get me.

—Tom Wilson, "Ziggy"

Never argue with a doctor; he has inside information.

—Bob and Ray

Never go to a doctor whose office plants are dead.

—Erma Bombeck

(Patient to doctor) But if I'm a hypochondriac, how will I know when I really do get sick?

—From a cartoon by McCotic

Be suspicious of any doctor who tries to take your temperature with his finger.

—David Letterman

My doctor says I need a complete change—so I'm changing my doctor.

—Edmund Orrin

My doctor likes to break things to me gently. The other day I asked him, "Doc, is it serious?" He said, "Only if you have plans for next year!"

—**Robert Orben**

My doctor, Nick the Knife, is a specialist . . . he specializes in cutting up my knees and sticking needles into me. And he's really painless—he doesn't feel any pain at all.

—**Joe Namath**

A friend of mine went to the doctor about a ringing in his ear. The doctor gave him an unlisted ear.

—**Charlie Callas**

All them surgeons—they're highway robbers. Why do you think they wear masks when they work on you?

—**Archie Bunker, "All in the Family"**

Dreams

My father never lived to see his dream come true of an all-Yiddish-speaking Canada.

—**David Steinberg**

If dreaming is all your subconscious desires coming out, why do people wait until they're asleep to do it?

—**Max Headroom, "Max Headroom"**

Last night I dreamt I had insomnia. When I woke up, I was completely exhausted but too well rested to go back to sleep.

—Bob Nickman

Drinking

I envy people who drink—at least they know what to blame everything on.

—Oscar Levant

I haven't touched a drop of alcohol since the invention of the funnel.

—Malachy McCourt

I've never been drunk, but often I've been overserved.

—George Gobel

I have a very good reason for bein' loaded tonight. I been drinkin' all day!

—Foster Brooks

Most people hate the taste of beer to begin with. It is, however, a prejudice that many people have been able to overcome.

—Winston Churchill

49

Even though a number of people have tried, no one has yet to find a way to drink for a living.

—Jean Kerr

You're sucked into drinking beer by believing it's a healthy thing! All these commercials show manly men doing manly things. "You've just killed a small animal . . . it's time for a light beer." Why not have realistic commercials? "It's 4 A.M., you've just pissed in a dumpster—it's Miller time."

—Robin Williams

What is the point of nonalcoholic beer? This must be for people who *don't* want to get drunk, but *do* want to spend the entire evening in the bathroom peeing their brains out!

—Marsha Doble

The worst beer I ever had was wonderful.

—Robert B. Parker (Spenser in *Mortal Stakes*)

Beer will make you see things that aren't there—like an attractive woman.

—Derrick Cameron

I had a few drinks last night. When I went to bed, the room was spinning—and then it stopped and I was thrown out the window.

—Jim Tavare

One more drink and I'll be under the host.

—Dorothy Parker

Driving

If your wife wants to learn to drive, don't stand in her way.

—**Sam Levenson**

Anybody in the audience with New York license plate BL75836745895947362047565, will you kindly move it? Your license plate is blocking traffic.

—**Bill Dana**

Since 1952 I wanted to drive a Caddy. And that's what I drive now—a '52 Caddy.

—**Bob Melvin**

I was stopped once for going 53 in a 35 mph zone, but I told them I had dyslexia.

—**Spanky McFarland**

If you don't want to get a ticket, just pick your nose when the cops pull up next to you. They won't give you a ticket because you have to sign it with their pen.

—**Denny Johnson**

If I was a cop, I'd hang out at the 7-Eleven to catch drunk drivers. If you see a guy stagger in and order one of those burritos at three in the morning, you have probable cause right there!

—**Mark Cordes**

I did the traffic at a very very small-town radio station. The the whole report was one sentence: "The light is green."

—**Jim Patterson**

In most states you can get a driver's license when you're sixteen years old, which made a lot of sense to me when I was sixteen years old but now seems insane.

—**Dave Barry**

Stuff a garlic clove in your shorts, and when your carpool shows up, sit in the middle.

—**Howard Albrecht and Sheldon Keller**

If most auto accidents happen within five miles of home, why don't we move ten miles away?

—**Michael Davis**

Drugs

I used to do drugs. I got so wrecked one night, I waited for a stop sign to change—and it did.

—**Steve Krabitz**

We've narrowed it down. We know they're bringing drugs in three ways: by air, by sea, and by land. But other than those three routes, we've got 'em beat.

—**Tom Mock**

Cocaine is God's way of telling you, you have too much money.

—**Robin Williams**

You wanna see drug-related violence—ban cigarettes in the United States.

—**Marsha Doble**

If God wanted us high, He would have given us wings.

—**Arsenio Hall**

If everyone took tranquilizers, no one would need them!

—**Edmund Orrin**

People who get stoned try and get their animals stoned, too. It's not bad enough that you proved Darwin was wrong . . . you have to take the whole family with you.

—**Robin Williams**

Smoking is, as far as I'm concerned, the entire point of being an adult.

—**Fran Lebowitz**

How can a kid ten years old find a dope pusher and the FBI can't?

—**Red Skelton**

The Economy

If all economists were laid end to end, they would not reach a conclusion.

—**George Bernard Shaw**

On this day in 1915, Buffalo Bill Cody said, "I'm going to a State Dinner tonight—what do you wear to a recession?"

—**Sheldon Keller**

Frankly, I'm worried about the economy. Yesterday, my neighbor ran out of money. That may not seem serious to you, but I live next door to a bank!

—**Robert Orben**

You can tell the economy is improving. Two more raises and my take-home pay will equal my deductions.

—**Slappy White**

George Bush said he returned the Haitian refugees because he didn't want to open our doors to economic refugees from all over the world. You see, under his domestic program, I guess he figures we can produce enough economic refugees right here at home.

—**Jay Leno**

One good thing about inflation is that the fellow who forgets his change nowadays doesn't lose half as much as he used to.

—**Kin Hubbard**

Once the people in all countries start having their noses fixed, the economy in those countries will really zoom. Plastic surgery is not cheap.

—Selma Diamond

A study of economics usually reveals that the best time to buy anything is last year.

—Marty Allen

Education

College is the best time of your life. When else are your parents going to spend several thousand dollars a year just for you to go to a strange town and get drunk every night?

—David Wood

I majored in nursing. I had to drop it, 'cause I ran out of milk.

—Judy Tenuta

I have a daughter who goes to SMU. She could've gone to UCLA, but it's one more letter she'd have to remember.

—Shecky Greene

I went to a high school that was so dangerous, the school newspaper had an obituary column.

—Rocky Ray

I'm enjoying summer school. I believe it's been good for me—and it saves a lot of sunscreen.

—Peppermint Patty in "Peanuts" by Charles Schulz

I worked as a substitute teacher in the off-season. As far as I'm concerned, the only thing wrong with schools is children. Get rid of those kids, and you won't have any problems in the schools.

—Ron Luciano

I'd have scored higher on my SAT, but I was on steroids and kept breaking my pencil.

—From a cartoon by Cochran

The kids from fifteen countries took math and science tests. We came in fourteenth behind Slovenia, which has only been a country since Tuesday.

—Bill Maher

Next week I have to take my college aptitude test. In my high school, they didn't even teach aptitude.

—Tony Banta, "Taxi"

Studying literature at Harvard is like learning about women at the Mayo Clinic.

—Roy Blount, Jr.

Sex in the hands of public educators is not a pretty thing.

—Kevin Arnold, "The Wonder Years"

Ego

Well, enough about me. Let's talk about you. What do you think about me?

—**Bette Midler, in** *Beaches*

I'm so fast, that when I turn the light switch off in my bedroom, I'm in bed before the light goes off!

—**Muhammad Ali**

A lot of people may not know this, but I'm quite famous.

—**Sam Malone, "Cheers"**

The great ones are never recognized in their own lifetimes.

—**Slap Maxwell, "Slap Maxwell"**

I talk to myself because I like dealing with a better class of people.

—**Jackie Mason**

How come nobody wants to argue with me? Is it because I'm always right?

—**Jim Bouton, author of** *Ball Four*

A fan club is a group of people that tells an actor he's not alone in the way he feels about himself.

—**Jack Carson**

I can't wait until tomorrow, 'cause I get better looking every day.

—**Joe Namath**

Excuses

I'm not that bad; I'm just drawn that way.

—**Jessica Rabbit,** *Who Framed Roger Rabbit?*

I try not to have any ideas. It only leads to complications.

—**Johnny Fever, "WKRP in Cincinnati"**

Honesty is the best policy, but insanity is a better defense.

—**Steve Landesberg**

The devil made me do it!

—**Flip Wilson**

My teacher told me that today was the first day of the rest of my life. I said, "That explains why I didn't do yesterday's homework!"

—**Lorne Elliot**

Reality is the leading cause of stress amongst those in touch with it. I can take it in small doses—but, as a lifestyle, I find it too confining.

—**Trudy,** *The Search for Signs of Intelligent Life*, **by Jane Wagner**

Exit Lines

I once wanted to save the world. Now I just want to leave the room with some dignity.

—**Lotus Weinstock**

I wish I could stay longer, but my girlfriend's getting pregnant tonight and I'd like to be there when it happens.

—Teddy Bergeron

Excuse my dust.

—Dorothy Parker (epitaph, suggested by herself)

My Uncle Swanny was an angry man. He had printed on his grave: "What are you looking at?"

—Margaret Smith

Let's take time out for a few commercial messages while I think of something to say.

—Andy Rooney

Go, and never darken my towels again.

—Groucho Marx

I'll be right back.

—Johnny Carson (whenever asked what he'd like his epitaph to say)

I'm going to put on my gravestone: "I told you I was sick!"

—Spike Milligan

On the whole, I'd rather be in Philadelphia.

—W. C. Fields (his apocryphal epitaph)

In the end, everything is a gag.

—Charlie Chaplin

And away we go!

—Jackie Gleason

Good night, Mrs. Calabash, wherever you are.

—Jimmy Durante

Family

Having a family is like having a bowling alley installed in your brain.

—Martin Mull

The easiest way to have your family tree traced is to run for public office.

—Carolyn Coats

Never raise your hands to your kids. It leaves your groin unprotected.

—Red Buttons

My parents are both in their nineties, and I'm very fortunate they are still with me. They're not with me—they're in Florida—because if they were with me, I couldn't take them for ten minutes.

—Alan King

My ancestors go back to Columbus. In fact, some of them go back to Toledo.

—Lew Parker

Cleaning your house while your children are still growing is like shoveling the walk before it stops snowing.

—**Phyllis Diller**

Ah, home sweet hell.

—**Al Bundy, "Married with Children"**

Fashion

I base my fashion taste on whatever doesn't itch.

—**Gilda Radner**

I got some new underwear the other day. Well, new to me.

—**Emo Phillips**

The good thing about prison is that you never have to wonder what to wear.

—**Carol Siskind**

I'm not the best dresser. Every year Goodwill gives me five hundred dollars not to clean out my closets.

—**Pat Cooper**

What sets man apart from animals is his ability to accessorize.

—*Spy* **magazine**

Girls used to show a lot of style—today's styles show a lot of girl.

—**Lucille Ball**

When Eve said she had nothing to wear, she meant it!

—**Milton Berle**

Even when I know it isn't true, some little part of me always clings to the hope that everything would be different if I just had a new color of lipstick.

—**"Cathy," by Cathy Guisewite**

Clothes make the man. Naked people have little or no influence on society.

—**Mark Twain**

Feelings

We have nothing to fear but sanity itself.

—**Mork, "Mork and Mindy"**

I cried for the man with no hair, until I met the man with no head.

—**Bud Lutz**

I have mixed feelings about ambivalence.

—**Bob Nickman**

Fear is taking your kid to a beginning math class and recognizing the person sitting next to him as your tax accountant.

—Anon.

Hope is the feeling you have that the feeling you have isn't permanent.

—Jean Kerr

Food

Resist eating anything that when dropped on the floor excites a dog.

—Erma Bombeck

The trouble with eating Italian food is that five or six days later you're hungry again.

—George Miller

I had the new Chinese-German food recently. It tastes great, but an hour later you're hungry for POWER!

—Ron Ellis

A poor person came up to me and said, "I haven't eaten in two days." I said, "You should force yourself."

—Henny Youngman

(On his wife's cooking) How could toast have bones?

—**Rodney Dangerfield**

Why am I bothering to eat this chocolate? I might as well just apply it directly to my thighs.

—**Rhoda Morgenstern, "The Mary Tyler Moore Show"**

I went to a restaurant. It said, "Breakfast anytime." So I ordered French toast during the Renaissance.

—**Steven Wright**

Cauliflower is nothing but cabbage with a college education.

—**Mark Twain**

Never eat anything you can't pronounce.

—**Erma Bombeck**

In Mexico we have a word for sushi: bait.

—**José Simon**

I can't cook. I use a smoke alarm as a timer.

—**Carol Siskind**

I idolized my mother. I didn't realize she was a lousy cook until I went into the army.

—**Jackie Gayle**

An hors d'oeuvre is an unfamiliar creature curled up on a cracker and stabbed with a toothpick to make sure it's dead.

—**Pat Buttram**

It's been said that fish is a good brain food. That's a fallacy. But brains are a good fish food.

—Mel Brooks

According to statistics, a man eats a prune every twenty seconds. I don't know who this fellow is, but I know where to find him.

—Morey Amsterdam

I won't eat anything that has intelligent life, but I'd gladly eat a TV network executive or a politician.

—Marty Feldman

I'm a Volvo-vegetarian. I'll eat an animal only if it was accidentally killed by a speeding car.

—Ron Smith

No man is lonely while eating spaghetti. It requires too much attention.

—Christopher Morley

My wife broke our dog of begging at the table—she let him taste it.

—Pat Cooper

Next to jazz music, there is nothing that lifts the spirit and strengthens the soul more than a bowl of chili.

—Harry James

Mustard's no good without roast beef.

—Chico Marx, *Monkey Business*

Only dull people are brilliant at breakfast.

—**Oscar Wilde**

Nouvelle cuisine, roughly translated, means "I can't believe I spent ninety-six dollars and I'm still hungry!"

—**Mike Kalin**

Part of the secret of success in life is to eat what you like and let the food fight it out inside.

—**Mark Twain**

Frugality

Why pay a dollar for a bookmark? Why not just use the dollar as a bookmark?

—**Fred Stoller**

My father originated the limbo dance—trying to get into a pay toilet.

—**Slappy White**

When I lost my rifle, the army charged me eighty-five dollars. That's why in the navy the Captain goes down with the ship.

—**Dick Gregory**

I started out with nothing. I still have most of it.

—**Michael Davis**

God

God don't make no mistakes—that's how He got to be God.

—**Archie Bunker, "All in the Family"**

Every day people are straying away from the church and going back to God.

—**Lenny Bruce**

I fear that one day I'll meet God, He'll sneeze, and I won't know what to say.

—**Ronnie Shakes**

I didn't want to pray to God 'cause I didn't want Him to know where I was.

—**Marsha Doble**

I guess I began to doubt the existence of God after I had been married for about three years.

—**Brian Savage**

Christ died for our sins. Dare we make His martyrdom meaningless by not committing them?

—**Jules Feiffer**

I think God invented rain to give dead people something to complain about.

—**David Brenner**

How come when we talk to God, we're said to be praying, but when God talks to us, we're schizophrenic?

—**Lily Tomlin**

Government

I don't make jokes. I just watch the government and report the facts.

—**Will Rogers**

Crime wouldn't pay if we let the government run it.

—**Joey Adams**

I wrote to the FBI to ask if they had a file on me. They wrote back, "We do now."

—**James Tripp**

We're getting a lot of government these days, but we'd probably be worse off if we were getting as much as we're paying for.

—**Olin Miller**

What is a nonessential government worker? I guess it would be any government worker who doesn't drive a snow plow.

—"Shoe" by Jeff MacNelly

The business of government is to keep the government out of business—that is, unless business needs government aid.

—Will Rogers

Our government has thrown away about one hundred and fifty billion dollars on the Hubble space telescope. Already it has discovered a third moon over Neptune. I just wish I was there when they broke this news to the Ethiopian children just to see the smiles on their little faces.

—Teddy Bergeron

Grandparents

The reason grandparents and grandchildren get along so well is that they have a common enemy.

—Sam Levenson

I bought my grandmother a seeing-eye dog. But he's a little sadistic. He does impressions of cars screeching to a halt.

—Larry Amoros

My grandfather had a special rocking chair made so it would lean forward. He could feign interest in any conversation.

—Steven Wright

My grandmother, she started walking five miles a day when she was sixty. She's ninety-seven today—and we don't know where the hell she is.

—Ellen DeGeneres

It was in Russia that she perfected the grandmother's art of boiling all the flavor out of food.

—Billy Crystal

My grandfather's been senile all his life. But no one ever told me and I've been taking all his advice.

—Steve Sweeny

Health

My allergy tests suggest that I may have been intended for some other planet.

—Walt Wetterberg

The only way to keep your health is to eat what you don't want, drink what you don't like, and do things you'd rather not.

—Mark Twain

I have to exercise in the morning before my brain figures out what I'm doing.

—**Marsha Doble**

The only reason I would take up jogging is so that I could hear heavy breathing again.

—**Erma Bombeck**

Misery is being a smoker, and being chased by a mugger who isn't!

—**Unknown**

Did you ever see the customers in health-food stores? They are pale, skinny people who look half dead. In a steak house, you see robust, ruddy people. They're dying, of course, but they look terrific.

—**Bill Cosby**

I'm not into working out. My philosophy: No pain, no pain.

—**Carol Leifer**

It's no longer a question of staying healthy. It's a question of finding a sickness you like.

—**Jackie Wilson**

I don't jog. If I die, I want to be sick.

—**Abe Lemons**

If you look like your passport photo, you're too ill to travel.

—**Will Kommen**

If you haven't any charity in your heart, you have the worst kind of heart trouble.

—**Bob Hope**

Hecklers

I don't mind hecklers, because I know how to ignore people—I was an airline stewardess.

—**Jo-Ann Deering**

Now you know why some animals eat their young.

—**Cork Proctor**

It's kind of silly to heckle. You've spent big money to see the show, and you're ruining it for yourself. It's like going to the ballet and trying to trip the dancers.

—**Jimmy Brogan**

Sir, were your parents brother and sister?

—**Cork Proctor**

When your IQ gets to 80, sell.

—**Unknown**

Shut up. I don't go to where you work and unplug the Slurpee machine.

—**Unknown**

My dear sir, I quite agree with you. But who are we among so many?

—George Bernard Shaw

History

It's a known fact that every major dictator in history was a morning person.

—A. Whitney Brown

The Soviet Union was bound to fall. It was all the way on the edge of the map.

—Kelly Bundy, "Married with Children"

Nixon, Ford, Carter, Reagan—a Mount Rushmore of incompetence.

—David Steinberg

George Washington said to his father, "If I never tell a lie, how can I get to be president?"

—Red Buttons

Abraham Lincoln always said, "You can't fool all of the people all of the time." But Abe Lincoln was fooling when he said that!

—Mark Russell

Never brag about your ancestors coming over on the *Mayflower*; the immigration laws weren't as strict in those days.

—**Lew Lehr**

Most people don't know that while Paul Revere was out yelling, "The British are coming!" his wife was home making sure of it!

—**Ron Ellis**

In ancient times they sacrificed the virgins. Men were not about to sacrifice the sluts.

—**Bill Maher**

Huh?

CBS Chairman Bill Paley came into our dressing room, opened a bottle of champagne, poured the glasses, and said, "Bottoms up!" I said, "Isn't that an awkward position for drinking?"

—**Gracie Allen**

I'm a peripheral visionary. I can see into the future but *way* off to the side."

—**Steven Wright**

I couldn't be out of money. I still have checks.

—**Attributed to Gracie Allen**

An oral contract is not worth the paper it's written on!

—**Samuel Goldwyn**

I hate when my foot falls asleep during the day, because I know it's going to be awake all night.

—**Steven Wright**

I heard a woman ask the doctor if it was okay to have children after thirty-five. I said, "Thirty-five children is enough for any woman."

—**Gracie Allen**

People in hell, where do they tell people to go?

—**Red Skelton**

I'm real forgetful. As I was driving over here, all of a sudden I thought, "Oh no, where are my car keys?"

—**Paul Dillery**

I got nothin' against mankind. It's people I can't stand.

—**Archie Bunker, "All in the Family"**

You've buttered your bread, now sleep in it.

—**Gracie Allen**

Humor

The saving grace of humor: If you fail, at least you don't have anyone laughing at you.

—**A. Whitney Brown**

Comedy is the blues for people who can't sing.

—**Chris Rock**

I'd like to tell you some jokes now, but you'd only laugh.

—**Milton Berle**

The quickest way to be funny is sleep with a lot of funny people.

—**Penny Marshall**

You have to come up with a funny idea a day for the rest of your life. Then you have to execute it in twenty-five words or less, in a small space.

—**Nancy N. Colelis, on being a cartoonist**

We're young only once—but with humor, we can be immature forever.

—**Art Gliwer**

When you do comedy (versus drama), you feel you're not eating at the adult table.

—**Jerry Seinfeld**

One doesn't have a sense of humor. It has you.

—**Larry Gelbart**

Improvisation is just writing in front of an audience.

—**Carl Reiner**

Humor is the shortest distance between two people.

—**Victor Borge**

Everything is funny as long as it's happening to somebody else.

—**Will Rogers**

Everything human is pathetic. The secret source of humour itself is not joy but sorrow. There is no humour in heaven.

—**Mark Twain**

Insults

I saw the play at a disadvantage. The curtain was up.

—**George S. Kaufman**

If you ever become a mother, can I have one of the puppies?

—**Charles Pierce**

I just want to say—if you had lived, you would have been a very sick man.

—**Jack E. Leonard**

This movie director has given us so many turkeys, he should be made an honorary Pilgrim!

—**Gene Shalit**

They say you shouldn't say nothin' about the dead unless it's good. He's dead. Good!

—**Moms Mabley**

He paid me a compliment. He said I looked like a breath of fresh spring. Well, he didn't actually use them words. He actually said I looked like the end of a hard winter.

—Minnie Pearl

International Relations

Iraq attacks Kuwait, there's an upheaval in Liberia, there's an attempted coup in the Philippines. You get the feeling that the Goodwill Games just didn't work out last year.

—Jay Leno

(Wife to husband) The good news is that I saw Gorbachev in the supermarket. The bad news is that he took the last thirty-six cans of pork and beans.

—From a cartoon by Staysical

Those French have a different word for everything!

—Steve Martin

I'm in favor of liberalized immigration because of the effect it would have on restaurants. I'd let just about everybody in except the English.

—Calvin Trillin

France is the only country where the money falls apart and you can't tear the toilet paper.

—Billy Wilder

I took a speed-reading course and I read *War and Peace*. It involves Russia.

—**Woody Allen**

Irony

I have hair and yet I'm bald.

—**Bob Nickman**

My father invented the burglar alarm—which unfortunately was stolen from him.

—**Victor Borge**

The other day I bought a wastebasket and carried it home in a paper bag. And when I got home, I put the paper bag in the wastebasket!

—**Lily Tomlin**

If life was fair, Elvis would be alive and all the impersonators would be dead.

—**Johnny Carson**

Nobody liked me because I was too popular.

—**Jackie Vernon**

Our priorities are screwed up in this country. It's illegal for a terminally ill person to take their own life, but we let Evel Knievel jump the Grand Canyon on a moped . . . and we watch it on television.

—**Keith Robinson**

An Australian inventor was the first to combine a boomerang and a hand grenade. He was also the last.

—Henry Haverstock

How come Superman would stand there and deflect bullets with his chest, but when the bad guy ran out of bullets and threw the gun at him he would duck?

—Bobby Kelton

Midgets are the last to know it's raining.

—Larry Tucker

Lawyers

Broke a mirror in my house and I'm supposed to get seven years bad luck, but my lawyer thinks he can get me five.

—Steven Wright

Juries scare me. I don't want to put my faith in twelve people who weren't smart enough to get out of jury duty.

—Monica Piper

To save the state the expense of a trial, your honor, my client has escaped.

—Chon Day

My parents sent my brother through law school. Now he's suing them for wasting seven years of his life.

—**Lawyers Binder**

I recently was a cost analyst with the San Diego law firm of Dewy, Cheatum, and Howe.

—**Catherine O'Hara**

If law school is so tough, how come there are so many lawyers?

—**Calvin Trillin**

If you can't get a lawyer who knows the law, get one who knows the judge.

—**Unknown**

As a result of starvation pay in the sciences, the class of '91 will include 30,000 new lawyers who will soon be chasing ambulances and sifting through obstetric files eager to rob someone at the point of a pen.

—**A. Whitney Brown**

What kind of a crazy world is it when the only person we have to defend us is a lawyer?

—**Merrit Malloy**

If you can't get a lawyer to call you back, try not paying his bill.

—**Unnamed comic**

Love and Relationships

When you're in love, it's the most glorious two-and-a-half days of your life.

—Richard Lewis

When I met Jean, I felt God reach down out of the sky, pull my hair, and say, "This one, dummy!"

—Richard Atcheson

Once the trust goes out of a relationship, it's really no fun lying to 'em anymore.

—Norm Peterson, "Cheers"

Frank Sinatra and I are such good friends that he always makes me walk in front of him if we're in a big crowd or heavy traffic.

—Don Rickles

I told you one hundred and fifty-eight times I cannot stand little notes on my pillow. "We are out of cornflakes. F.U." It took me three hours to figure out F.U. was Felix Ungar.

—Oscar Madison, *The Odd Couple*, by Neil Simon

I don't mind women leaving me, but they tell you *why*!

—Richard Pryor

I broke up with my girlfriend. She moved in with another guy, and I draw the line at that.

—Garry Shandling

I'm very single. I was going with someone for a few years, but we broke up. It was one of those things. He wanted to get married. And I didn't want him to.

—Rita Rudner

We never get sick of each other. That's how sick we are.

—Roseanne Barr-Arnold (on her relationship with Tom Arnold)

She bad-mouthed me when we broke up. She said I faked foreplay.

—Richard Lewis

I can't get a relationship to last longer than it takes to make copies of their tapes.

—Margaret Smith

My girlfriend told me that she was seeing another man. I told her to rub her eyes.

—Emo Phillips

Dr. Ruth says that, as women, we should tell our lovers how to make love to us. My boyfriend goes nuts if I tell him how to drive!

—Pam Stone

You meet someone and you're sure you were lovers in a past life. After two weeks with them, you realize why you haven't kept in touch for the last two thousand years.

—Al Cleathen

That's your idea of a romantic dinner, Oscar? Red wine and fish sticks?

—**Felix Ungar, "The Odd Couple"**

I think—therefore, I'm single.

—**Lizz Winstead**

Marriage

I will not cheat on my wife—because I love my house.

—**Chas Elstner**

The difference between my wife and my mistress is the difference between night and day.

—**Harry Hirshfield**

Trust your husband, adore your husband, and get as much as you can in your own name.

—**Joan Rivers**

Marriage is like the Middle East—no solutions.

—*Shirley Valentine*

Married men live longer than single men, but married men are a lot more willing to die.

—**Johnny Carson**

The bride was pregnant, so everyone threw puffed rice!

—**Dick Cavett**

I've been married fourteen years, and I have three kids. Obviously, I breed well in captivity.

—**Roseanne Barr-Arnold**

Before marriage, a man will lie awake all night thinking about something you said—after marriage, he'll fall asleep before you finish saying it.

—**Geraldo Rivera**

Marriage starts with billing and cooing, but only the billing lasts.

—**Henny Youngman**

The man who criticizes his wife's taste is apt to overlook the fact that she picked him for a husband.

—**Unknown**

We want playmates we can own.

—**Jules Feiffer**

When my wife and I made love, we always took the phone off the hook. When I was on the road, I called home at midnight, and the line was busy.

—**Rodney Dangerfield**

Bachelors know more about women than married men. If they didn't, they'd be married too!

—**H. L. Mencken**

My wife and I were happy for twenty years. Then we met.

—**Rodney Dangerfield**

My wife and I just celebrated out twelfth anniversary. I'm Catholic, so there's no real possibility of divorce. I'm Irish—so there *is* the possibility of murder.

—**J. J. Wall**

My wife thinks I'm too nosy. At least that's what she writes in her diary.

—**Drake Sathe**

I had five years of happy marriage, which is not bad out of fifteen.

—**Bob Thomas**

Marriage is like a bank account. You put it in, you take it out, you lose interest.

—**Professor Irwin Corey**

It is better to have loved and lost than to have loved and married.

—**Sammy Shore**

My wife converted me to religion. I never believed in hell until I married her.

—**Hal Roach**

Before marriage, a girl has to make love to her man to hold him; after marriage, she has to hold him to make love to him.

—**Marilyn Monroe**

At a wedding you never hear a man clearly say, "I do," because we figure we can get out of it later on a technicality.

—**Sinbad**

My husband Al has trouble saying the little things like, "I love you," "You're beautiful," and "Look out, a car is coming."

—Peg Bundy, "Married with Children"

After you've been married for a while, the women will start choosing your clothes. If you protest, they'll say: "Dressing is a privilege. You abused it, and now you've lost it."

—Cary Long

Men

To women, we are like big dogs that talk.

—Larry Miller

Men have a much better time of it than women; for one thing, they marry later; for another thing, they die earlier.

—H. L. Mencken

I'm looking for a perfume to overpower men—I'm sick of karate.

—Phyllis Diller

A feminist man is like a jumbo shrimp. Neither makes any sense.

—Cassandra Davis

I only like two kinds of men: domestic and foreign.

—**Mae West**

Show me a man with both feet on the ground, and I'll show you a man who can't put his pants on.

—**Joe E. Lewis**

A man is as old as the women he feels.

—**Groucho Marx**

When I think of some of the men I've slept with—if they were women, I wouldn't have had lunch with them.

—**Carol Siskind**

Men are no good at playing dumb because most of the time they're not playing.

—**Larry Miller**

Don't let a man put anything over on you except an umbrella.

—**Mae West**

If man had created man, he would be ashamed of his performance.

—**Mark Twain**

Eventually, all men come out of the bathroom dressed as a majorette.

—**Ernestyne White**

If you women knew what we were thinking, you'd never stop slapping us.

—**Larry Miller**

If anything happens to me, tell every woman I've ever gone out with I was talking about her at the end. That way, they'll have to reevaluate me.

—Albert Brooks to Holly Hunter in *Broadcast News*

Men are nothing but lazy lumps of drunken flesh. They crowd you in bed, get you all worked up, and then before you can say, "Is that all there is?" that's all there is.

—Latka Gravas's mother, "Taxi"

Can you imagine a world without men? No crime and lots of happy fat women.

—Marion Smith

Military

I was almost drafted. Luckily, I was wounded while taking the physical.

—Jackie Mason

It's always sad when a ten-year-old gets drawn into war.

—Matt Groening, creator of "The Simpsons," commenting on Defense Secretary Dick Cheney's flaunting of a Bart Simpson doll in camouflage

How can we have an invasion when the troops storm ashore and they then change their minds.

—Bob Hope (on women in combat)

89

Ze soldiers are very happy shooting ze pipples who say that ze pipples are not happy.

—**George Hamilton,** *Zorro, the Gay Blade*

I think war might be God's way of teaching us geography.

—**Paul Rodriguez**

Go to war. Keep the world safe for hypocrisy."

—**"Laugh-In"**

Money

Money is not everything, but it is better than having one's health.

—**Woody Allen**

When this deal is completed, gentlemen, we'll never have to worry about money again. Instead, we'll probably have to worry about going to jail.

—**From a cartoon in** *Punch*

I have enough money to last me the rest of my life—unless I buy something.

—**Jackie Mason**

You can try to ask your congressman for help, but don't accept his check.

—**Opening rap number for "Comic Relief V"**

There is no money in poetry, but then there is no poetry in money either.

—**Robert Graves**

The only way to double your money in Las Vegas is to mug somebody at the airport and get on an airplane and come on back home.

—**George Wallace**

I've got all the money I'll ever need—if I die by four o'clock.

—**Henny Youngman**

I'm going to start living within my means—even if I have to get a loan to do it.

—**Tom Wilson, "Ziggy"**

Our government has said that Americans are geographically illiterate and economically ignorant. It's true. How many times have you said to yourself, "Where did all my money go?"

—**Alan Prophet**

Money really isn't everything. If it was, what would we buy with it?

—**Tom Wilson, "Ziggy"**

Money can't buy love—but it certainly puts you in a wonderful bargaining position.

—**Harrison Baker**

Money is a good thing to have. It frees you from doing things you dislike. Since I dislike doing nearly everything, money is handy.

—**Groucho Marx**

Nature

All modern humans are descended from a wormlike creature, but it shows more on some people.

—Will Cuppy

Ants can carry twenty times their own body weight, which is useful information if you're moving out and you need help getting a potato chip across town.

—Ron Darian

I was making love to my wife this morning when the damned earthquake woke her up.

—Phil Harris

I have a seashell collection; maybe you've seen it? I keep it on beaches all over the world.

—Steven Wright

An earthquake is God grabbing the earth and saying, "Cough."

—Richard Belzer

High insurance rates are what really killed the dinosaurs.

—David Letterman

I like living out here. Earthquakes freaked me out; the first one actually helped me, though. I was bowling at the time.

—Henry Cho

I have a feeling our descendants are going to look back at all this nuclear hysteria from the bottom of their toxic-waste dumps and laugh their feelers off.

—A. Whitney Brown

Parents

It is not easy being a mother. If it were easy, fathers would do it.

—Dorothy, "The Golden Girls"

What is it about American fathers as they grow older that makes them dress like flags from other countries?

—Cary Odes

My mother was an authority on pigsties. "This is the worst-looking pigsty I have ever seen in my life, and I want it cleaned up right now."

—Bill Cosby

My father had three jobs and went to school at night. . . . If I go to the cleaners and the bank in the same day . . . I need a nap.

—Larry Miller

I think I'd be a good mother—maybe a little overprotective. Like I would never let the kid out—of my body!

—Wendy Liebman

It's almost impossible to refuse second helpings of food from an Italian lady like my mom. I used to brief my friends: "If you want a lot more food, smile at her. If you want just a little more, say 'No, I can't eat a thing.' If you don't want any more . . . you'll have to shoot her."

—**Ray Romano**

My father never took me to the zoo. He said, if they want me, they'll come get me.

—**Rodney Dangerfield**

I'm very protective of my daughters. "No, Jenny isn't home right now; she's on the space shuttle."

—**Billy Crystal**

My dad's pants kept creeping up on him. By sixty-five he was just a pair of pants and a head.

—**Jeff Altman**

My mother is against abortion for another reason. . . . She doesn't feel it's fair to kill the fetus and let the father live.

—**John DeBillis**

I was raised by just my mom. See, my father died when I was eight years old. At least that's what he told us in the letter.

—**Drew Carey**

I grew up to have my father's looks, my father's speech patterns, my father's posture, my father's walk, my father's opinions, and my mother's contempt for my father.

—**Jules Feiffer**

I am your father. I brought you into this world, and I can take you out.

—**Cliff Huxtable, "The Bill Cosby Show"**

Philosophy

When you study philosophy in school, you remember just enough to screw you up for the rest of your life.

—Steve Martin

I got an "A" in philosophy because I proved that my professor didn't exist.

—Judy Tenuta

I have a new philosophy. I am only going to dread one day at a time.

—Charles Schulz

As long as the world keeps turning and spinning, we're gonna be dizzy, and we're gonna make mistakes.

—Mel Brooks

What do we know about the beyond? Do we know what's behind the beyond? I'm afraid some of us hardly know what's beyond the behind.

—Brother Theodore

Have you ever wondered if illiterate people get the full effect of alphabet soup?

—John Mendoza

I guess I wouldn't believe in anything if it wasn't for my lucky astrology mood watch.

—Steve Martin

I think I am, therefore I am, I think.

—**Sister Mary Tricky**

I reek, therefore I am.

—**Diane, "Cheers"**

Politics

The only reason I'm not running for president is I'm afraid no woman would come forth and say she slept with me.

—**Garry Shandling**

Artificial hearts are nothing new. Politicians have had them for years.

—**Mack McGinnis**

The public is very fickle, as I was saying to my cab driver, Gerald Ford.

—**Pat McCormick**

The liberals can understand everything but people who don't understand them.

—**Lenny Bruce**

Congressional terms should be . . . ten to twenty with no possibility of parole.

—**Walt Handelsman**

The only way to combat criminals is by not voting for them.

—Dayton Allen

Liberals feel unworthy of their possessions . . . conservatives feel they deserve everything they've stolen.

—Mort Sahl

You can lead a man to Congress, but you can't make him think.

—Milton Berle

Liberals don't want to kill anything. They want the Listerine ads to say, "Rehabilitate the germs that can cause bad breath."

—Marc Price

When I was in the third grade, there was a kid running for office. His slogan was: "Vote for me and I'll show you my wee-wee." He won by a landslide.

—Dorothy, "The Golden Girls"

If Patrick Henry thought taxation without representation was bad, he should see it with representation!

—Unknown

Alfred E. Neuman runs for president with the slogan "You could do worse, and always have!"

—Jean Seligmann

We have a presidential election coming up. And I think the big problem, of course, is that someone will win.

—Barry Crimmins

I've made fun of seven presidents in my career, and I'm not about to stop now—especially when it's easy.

—**Alan King**

As far as the men who are running for president are concerned, they aren't even people I would date.

—**Nora Ephron**

A new poll showed that if the election was held today, people would be confused because it's usually held in November.

—**Kevin Nealon**

If God had wanted us to vote, he would have given us candidates.

—**Jay Leno**

I stand by my misstatements.

—**Dan Quayle**

Money can't buy happiness but it will certainly get you a better class of memories.

—**Ronald Reagan**

Psychology

Psychiatry tells us that one out of every five people is completely disturbed. And the reason is that the other four are nuts.

—**Dave Astor**

I went into a bookstore and asked the woman behind the counter where the self-help section was. She said, "If I told you that, it would defeat the whole purpose."

—**Brian Kiley**

After twelve years of therapy, my psychiatrist said something that brought tears to my eyes. He said, *"No hablo inglés."*

—**Ronnie Shakes**

I'm going to my psychoanalyst one more year, then I'm going to Lourdes.

—**Woody Allen**

After a year of therapy, my psychiatrist said to me, "Maybe life isn't for everyone."

—**Larry Brown**

We have met the enemy and he is us.

—"Pogo," by Walt Kelly

Roses are red, violets are blue. I'm schizophrenic and so am I.

—Frank Crow

Puns

The pun is the lowest form of humor, especially when you don't think of it first.

—Oscar Levant

It's as easy to get drunk on water—as it is on dry land."

—George Gobel

People in the monogram business achieve initial success!

—Norm Crosby

You show me a sculptor who works in the basement, and I'll show you a low-down chiseller.

—Soupy Sales

You can lead a horticulture but you can't make her think!

—Dorothy Parker

Thomas Edison put lights in all the outhouses on Indian reservations. Don't ever forget, he was the first man to wire a head for a reservation.

—**Norm Crosby**

Fascinate: There were nine buttons on her nightgown, but she could only fascinate.

—**Homer Haynes**

My brother, Harpo, rarely spoke, but when he did you could hear a pun drop.

—**Groucho Marx**

My father crossed a crow with a cuckoo. He got a raven maniac.

—**Jay Johnson**

Questions

What's another word for "thesaurus"?

—**Steven Wright**

Why is it that people in record stores act like they're rock'n' roll stars?

—**Barry Crimmins**

Who invented the brush they put next to the toilet? That thing hurts!

—**Andy Andrews**

If you shoot a mime, should you use a silencer?

—**Steven Wright**

What do the partners in a co-dependent couple say to each other? "That was wonderful for you. How was it for me?"

—**Wendy Kaminer**

Recovery

Beverly Hills AA: Hi, my name is Sid. I represent Bob; he's an alcoholic.

—**"Sid"**

Denial is not a river in Egypt.

—**AA axiom**

I joined Liars Anonymous, but I had a lot of trouble finding them because they put the wrong address in all their ads.

—**J. J. Waugh**

I'm so co-dependent, I have to ask my friends if I'm having a good time.

—**Unknown comic**

Religion

When I was a kid, I used to pray every night for a new bicycle. Then I realized that the Lord, in his wisdom, didn't work that way. So I just stole one and asked him to forgive me.

—Emo Phillips

Who do atheists talk to during sex?

—Karen Chatelle

They have Dial-a-Prayer for atheists now. You can call up and it rings and rings and nobody answers.

—Tommy Blaze

At the airport, these religious fanatics keep sticking these pins on me and asking, "Do you believe in God?" and I say, "I hope so because I'm a hemophiliac."

—Rick Overton

Rules, Laws, and Theorems

The Law of Raspberry Jam: The wider any culture is spread, the thinner it gets.

—Alvin Toffler

Soderquist's Paradox: There are more horses' asses than horses.

—John Peers

No problem is so big or so complicated that it can't be run away from.

—Linus, in "Peanuts," by Charles Schulz

Everything comes to him who waits. Except a loaned book.

—Kin Hubbard

There's no present. There's only the immediate future and the recent past.

—George Carlin

A man with one watch knows what time it is. A man with two watches is never sure.

—John Peers

God shows his contempt for wealth by the kind of person he selects to receive it.

—Austin O'Malley

The secret of staying young is to live honestly, eat slowly, and lie about your age.

—Lucille Ball

If you want to catch trout, don't fish in a herring barrel.

—Ann Landers

Never buy a fur from a vegetarian.

—Joan Rivers

The big print giveth and the small print taketh away.

—**Bishop Fulton J. Sheen**

The human brain starts working the moment you are born and never stops until you stand up to speak in public.

—**George Jessel**

Sayings

You can lead a herring to water, but you have to walk really fast or they die.

—**Rose Nylund, "The Golden Girls"**

Thomas Edison said that genius is one percent inspiration and ninety-nine percent perspiration. I hate to think of anyone that sweaty handling electricity.

—**Unknown**

You can't have everything. Where would you put it?

—**Steven Wright**

The meek shall inherit the earth. They won't have the nerve to refuse it.

—**Jackie Vernon**

A day without sunshine is like night.

—**Steve Martin**

There is a thin line between genius and insanity. I have erased this line.

—Oscar Levant

I am just minutes ahead of my time.

—Lotus Weinstock

That's the trouble with "Have a nice day!" It puts all the pressure on you.

—George Carlin

Have a day.

—Sister Mary Tricky

Self-Esteem

When I was born, my father spent three weeks trying to find a loophole in my birth certificate.

—Jackie Vernon

I have low self-esteem. When we were in bed together, I would fantasize I was someone else.

—Richard Lewis

Did you ever feel like the world's a tuxedo, and you're a pair of brown shoes?

—**George Gobel**

I don't think my parents liked me . . . my bathtub toys were a toaster and a blender!

—**Rodney Dangerfield**

I wouldn't belong to any club that would have me as a member!

—**Groucho Marx**

My Uncle Naibob wasn't a failure. He just started out at the bottom and liked it there.

—**Minnie Pearl**

I would get into bed and my girlfriend would mentally dress me.

—**Richard Lewis**

My twin brother forgot my birthday.

—**Rip Taylor**

If you think nobody cares if you're alive, try missing a couple of car payments.

—**Earl Wilson**

I never know how much of what I say is true.

—**Bette Midler**

Underneath this flabby exterior is an enormous lack of character.

—**Oscar Levant**

I made quite a name for myself back home. I left when I found out what that name was!

—**Herb Shriner**

Dial-a-Prayer hung up on me.

—**Jackie Vernon**

In my youth I wanted to be a great pantomimist, but I found I had nothing to say.

—**Victor Borge**

I wouldn't mind being the last man on earth—just to see if all those girls were telling me the truth.

—**Ronnie Shakes**

Sex

Remember when "Safe Sex" meant your parents had gone away for the weekend?

—**Rhonda Hansome**

I practice safe sex. I use an airbag.

—**Garry Shandling**

Safe sex is very important. That's why I'm never doing it on a plywood scaffolding again.

—**Jenny Jones**

I'm scared of sex now. You have to be. You can get something terminal, like a kid.

—**Wendy Liebman**

I think that's what we fought most about—our sex life. I wanted one!

—**Kip Addotta**

One night I made love for an hour and five minutes. It was the day they pushed the clock ahead.

—**Garry Shandling**

Who would have ever thought you could die from sex? It was much more fun when you only went to hell.

—**John Waters**

The only difference between sex and death is, with death you can do it alone and nobody's going to make fun of you.

—**Woody Allen**

The wonderful thing about celibacy is that you don't have to bother reading the manual.

—**Sheldon Keller**

The reason people sweat is so they don't catch fire when making love.

—Don Rose

When turkeys mate, they think of swans.

—Johnny Carson

Last time I made love to my wife nothing was happening, so I said to her, "What's the matter? You can't think of anybody else either?"

—Rodney Dangerfield

You sleep with a guy once, and, before you know it, he wants to take you to dinner.

—Myers Yori

It's stupid to be jealous of your partner's past. That's none of your business. I know Lisa had sex before we met. I can handle that. Of course, she didn't enjoy it.

—Rick Reynolds

If I believed in casual sex, I'd have stayed married.

—Marsha Doble

The closest I ever came to a ménage à trois was one time when I was dating a schizophrenic.

—Rita Rudner

For a single woman, the most effective method of oral contraception is to just yell out, "*Yes, yes,* I want to have your *baby!!!*"

—Marsha Doble

It's the good girls who keep the diaries; the bad girls never have the time.

—Tallulah Bankhead

Women need a reason to have sex, men just need a place.

—Billy Crystal

My wife said her wildest sexual fantasy would be if I got my own apartment.

—Rodney Dangerfield

Every night I slept with a strange girl. Same girl—she was just strange!

—Michael Davis

I want a good girl . . . and I want her bad.

—Donald McGill

They say the best exercise takes place in the bedroom. I believe it, because that's where I get the most resistance.

—Jeff Shaw

I can remember the night I lost my innocence in the back seat of the family car. It would have been more memorable if I hadn't been alone!

—Red Buttons

It is better to have loved and lost than to have paid for it and not liked it.

—Hiram Kasten

I was recently making love with a girl at 2 A.M., and she told me that I needed to go to a sex clinic. She said I should go right away, and ask for the emergency room.

—Mike Preminger

My wife insists on turning off the light when it's time for us to make love. That doesn't bother me. It's the hiding that seems so cruel.

—**Jonathan Katz**

There are so many sex magazines on the newsstands, I'm taking a course in speed-looking.

—**Earl Wilson**

My shorts have more ambition than I do.

—**Alex Reiger, "Taxi"**

If sex is so personal, why are we expected to share it with someone else?

—**Lily Tomlin**

Show Business

Give me a couple of years, and I'll make that actress an overnight success!

—**Samuel Goldwyn**

Show people tend to treat their finances like their dentistry. They assume the man handling it knows what he is doing.

—**Dick Cavett**

Changing agents is like changing deck chairs on the *Titanic*.

—**Judy Thomas**

Sports

Bat Day seems like a good idea, but I question the advisability of giving bats in the Bronx to forty thousand Yankee fans.

—**Aaron Bacall**

Tennis is like marrying for money. Love has nothing to do with it.

—**Phyllis Diller**

Baseball is different from politics. You're always out in baseball when you get caught stealing.

—**Unknown**

I competed in the long jump, because it seemed to be the only event where afterward you didn't fall down and throw up.

—**Dave Barry**

I could have played football for another two or three years. All I needed was a leg transplant.

—**John Unitas**

Golf is not a sport. Golf is men in ugly pants, walking.

—**Rosie O'Donnell**

If you watch a game, it's fun. If you play it, it's recreation. If you work at it, it's golf.

—**Bob Hope**

You know you're getting old when you start watching golf on TV and enjoying it.

—**Larry Miller**

Nolan Ryan is pitching much better now that he has his curve ball straightened out.

—**Joe Garagiola**

If you think it's hard to meet new people, trying picking up the wrong golf ball.

—**Jack Lemmon**

I've had a divorce, heart attack, and world championship all in one year—and I enjoyed them all.

—**John Bach, Assistant Coach of the Chicago Bulls**

The fascination of shooting as a sport depends on whether you are at the wrong end of the gun.

—**P. G. Wodehouse**

Anyone who likes golf on television would enjoy watching the grass grow on the greens.

—**Andy Rooney**

(About skiing) There's no need to go that fast without a plane around you.

—**Larry Miller**

I went skiing and I knew I was going too fast when I suddenly realized that I was actually getting younger.

—**John Ross**

Teenagers

Teenagers are hormones with feet.

—**Marsha Doble**

I don't think you should have to go to high school until you are at least forty, you've had lots of therapy, and you're ready for it.

—**Marilyn Kentz,** *Mommies*

Adolescence is just one big walking pimple.

—**Carol Burnett**

In short, the best thing to do is to behave in a manner befitting one's age. If you are sixteen and under, try not to go bald.

—**Woody Allen**

The trouble with the 1980s as compared with the 1970s is that teenagers no longer rebel and leave home.

—**Marion Smith**

Television

The answers to life's problems are not at the bottom of a bottle . . . ! They're on TV.

—**Homer Simpson**

Sequoias are turned into sequels, redwoods into remakes.

—**Larry Gelbart**

(One man to another) They will never really crack down on air pollution until it interferes with television reception.

—**From a cartoon by Capelini**

The only way you get any feeling out of your television set is if you touch it when you're wet.

—**Larry Gelbart**

My series was cancelled in spite of excellent ratings—one week we beat out "Let Us Pray."

—**Joey Bishop**

The state of the art is in a state of emergency.

—**Larry Gelbart**

Travel

You never appreciate your language until you go to a foreign country that doesn't have the *courtesy* to speak English.

—**Steve Martin**

The scientific theory I like best is that the rings of Saturn are composed entirely of lost airline luggage.

—**Mark Russell**

New York now leads the world's great cities in the number of people around whom you shouldn't make a sudden move.

—**David Letterman**

I flew to London on the Concorde. It goes faster than the speed of sound, which is fun. But it's a rip-off because you couldn't hear the movie until two hours after you got there.

—**Howie Mandel**

117

Santa Claus has the right idea: Visit people once a year.

—**Victor Borge**

I took an economy flight. There wasn't any movie, but they flew low over drive-ins.

—**Red Buttons**

(Tip to out-of-town visitors) If you buy something here in New York and you want to have it shipped home, be suspicious if the clerk tells you they don't need your name and address.

—**David Letterman**

I think I embarrassed the lady next to me on the plane. It was one of those flights that you sleep on, and I sleep in the nude.

—**Johnny Dark**

The airline people are always telling you that it's safer to fly than to drive. Why don't they tell you the other statistic—that it's safer to crash in a car than in a plane.

—**Brad Stein**

I flew here on one of those dinky commuter airlines. My plane was delayed 'cause it got caught in some kid's kite.

—**Keith Robinson**

If you like to spend your vacations in out-of-the-way places where few people go, let your wife read the map.

—**Jack Carter**

I took the vacation I wanted all my life. I packed Alice and the kids and all the luggage in the station wagon and headed it straight for Canada. Then I went to Las Vegas and had a ball.

—**George Gobel**

After the flight attendants tell about all the safety features, I always play a trick on them. I bring little ketchup packets and pour one just below each ear. Then I call the stewardess over, point to my ears and ask, "Is this supposed to happen?"

—**Brad Stein**

Truth

Truth is more of a stranger than fiction.

—**Mark Twain**

Always tell the truth; it's the world's best lie.

—**Uncle Martin, "My Favorite Martian"**

If you're going to tell people the truth, be funny or they'll kill you.

—**Billy Wilder**

I told them the truth and they fell for it.

—**Judge Harry Stone, "Night Court"**

When in doubt, tell the truth.

—**Mark Twain**

I never know how much of what I say is true.

—**Bette Midler**

Weight

I'm so fat that I've fallen down and not even known it.

—Pat McCormick

When you're not thin and blonde, you come up with a personality real quick.

—Kathy Najimy

I won't tell you how much I weigh, but don't get on the elevator with me unless you're going down.

—Jack E. Leonard

I got hit by a Volkswagen—and had to go to the hospital to have it removed.

—Pat McCormick

If I am ever stuck on a respirator or a life support system, I definitely want to be unplugged—but not until I get down to a size eight!

—Henriette Montel

You know you're too fat when you're standing next to your car and you get a ticket for double-parking.

—Totie Fields

She was so fat that he danced with her for half an hour before he realized she was sitting.

—Ed Wynn

Women

The bravest thing that men do is love women.

—Mort Sahl

I hate women because they always know where things are.

—James Thurber

Nothing spoils a romance so much as a sense of humour in a woman.

—Oscar Wilde

Women are the most powerful magnet in the universe. And all men are cheap metal, and we all know where North is.

—Larry Miller

Show me a woman who doesn't feel guilty, and I'll show you a man.

—Erica Jong

My idea of superwoman is someone who scrubs her own floors.

—Bette Midler

From birth to age eighteen, a girl needs good parents. From eighteen to thirty-five, she needs good looks. From thirty-five to fifty-five, she needs a good personality. From fifty-five on, she needs good cash.

—Sophie Tucker

I like American women. They do things sexually Russian girls would never dream of doing—like showering.

—Yakov Smirnoff

I'm just a person trapped inside a woman's body.

—Elayne Boosler

She contradicts me even when I don't say anything!

—Bill Hoest

Every time I find a girl who can cook like my mother, she looks like my father!

—Tony Randall

Men don't know much about women. We do know when they're happy, we know when they're crying, and we know when they're pissed off. We just don't know in what order these are gonna come at us.

—Evan Davis

Work

The easiest job in the world has to be a coroner. Surgery on dead people. What's the worst that can happen? If it all goes wrong . . . maybe you get a pulse.

—Dennis Miller

I like work; it fascinates me. I can sit and watch it for hours.

—**Jerome K. Jerome**

I lost my job. I didn't lose it—I know where it is—it's just when I go there, someone else is doing it.

—**Bobcat Goldthwaite**

A good rule of thumb is if you've made it to thirty-five and your job still requires you to wear a name tag, you've probably made a serious vocational error.

—**Dennis Miller**

I believe in the work ethic, just not the hard-work ethic.

—**From a cartoon by Cottiaon**

If you want successful workers, give them time enough to play.

—**John Cleese**

I've been out of work so long, I forget what kind of work I'm out of.

—**Robin Harris**

The trouble with unemployment is that the minute you wake up in the morning you're on the job.

—**Slappy White**

Writing

I'd like to pay tribute to my four writers: Matthew, Mark, Luke, and John.

—Bishop Fulton J. Sheen

Being a writer for Carol [Burnett] is like being a bat boy for Babe Ruth.

—Neil Simon

(A new regulation for the publishing industry) The advance for a book must be larger than the lunch at which it was discussed.

—Calvin Trillin

This is not a book to be tossed aside lightly. It should be thrown with great force.

—Dorothy Parker

Writing is easy. All you do is stare at a blank sheet of paper until drops of blood form on your forehead.

—Gene Fowler

The older I get, the less important the comma becomes. Let the reader catch his own breath.

—Elizabeth Clarkson Zwart

I'm working when I'm fighting with my wife. I constantly ask myself, ''How can I use this stuff to literary advantage?''

—Art Buchwald

Index

125